Fill in the Blanks
WITH MACHINE EMBROIDERY

REBECCA KEMP BRENT

©2007 Rebecca Kemp Brent
Published by

krause publications
An Imprint of F+W Publications

700 East State Street • Iola, WI 54990-0001
715-445-2214 • 888-457-2873
www.krausebooks.com

Our toll-free number to place an order or obtain
a free catalog is (800) 258-0929.

The following registered trademark terms and companies appear in this publication: Amazing Designs, Brother International, Buzz Tools, Coats & Clark, Crafter's Pride, Creative Design, Creative Machine Embroidery, DMC, Embroider This!, Hollywood Light, In the Hoop Designs, June Tailor, Madeira, Martha Pullen Company, McCalls Creates, Nature's Garden, Poly-fil, ScrapSMART, Sudberry House, Sulky, Walnut Hollow, The Warm Company, Wimpole Street, YLI, Zweigart.

Library of Congress Catalog Number: 2006939722

ISBN-13: 978-0-89689-483-9
ISBN-10: 0-89689-483-5

Edited by Andy Belmas
Designed by Lisa Kuhn, www.curiopress.com

Printed in China

Acknowledgments

My thanks are due to many wonderful, generous and talented individuals who have supported me in my career in general and while I was writing this book in particular. First, there are the three digitizers who agreed to work with me so that you will have a selection of wonderful embroidery designs to use as you experiment with blanks: Evy Hawkins, Shelly Smola and Sherry Titzer.

The shop owners and machine company executives who have given me a forum for teaching and developing ideas have contributed much more than machines, stabilizers and threads – not that those are unimportant! Thanks especially to Brother International and Floriani/ RNK Distributing for their ongoing support.

In addition, so many suppliers have provided blanks and materials for my use; please consult the Resources section at the end of the book and visit their locations as you make your own purchases.

Annette Bailey of "Creative Machine Embroidery" and Linda Griepentrog of G Wiz Creative Services have mentored me and provided the best of opportunities and friendship. As for Jonathan and Patricia, Mom and Dad: more thanks to you every day for all your love and support.

WHERE CREDIT IS DUE

Many talented digitizers and suppliers of wonderful blanks contributed to this book. The photos are accompanied by a credit line briefly listing the source or sources for the pictured blanks. If no source is noted, the blank was purchased from a local retailer, flea market or chain store, or drawn from the author's stash.

In addition, the embroidery design source is listed unless the pictured design(s) come from the enclosed CD-ROM. A more complete listing of blank and embroidery design credits can be found on the CD-ROM as well.

The pictured blanks were current at the time the book was written, and every effort has been made to ensure the blanks will continue to be available. However, manufacturers do change their product lines. If you are unable to find the exact blank pictured, contact the listed source or browse the suppliers listed under Resources on page 44 for alternatives.

A WORD ABOUT LETTERS

The monograms and lettering within these pages have come from a variety of sources. Some are listed in the Resources guide under Embroidery Designs, while others were digitized by the author using embroidery auto-digitizing software. Be encouraged to use any fonts from retail sources or lettering software to personalize the projects.

Introduction

This is a book for anyone with an embroidery machine, but it's especially dedicated to anyone who's embroidered a t-shirt or two – or a dozen – anyone who's ready to do something more with that fabulous machine and the amazing variety of embroidery designs available through local retailers and online stores.

Credit: Crafter's Pride, Nature's Garden, Embroider This!

So what IS a blank? It's anything that's unadorned, ready and waiting for a bit of embroidered embellishment. A blank may be as basic as those t-shirts, as special as an heirloom-quality linen tablecloth, or as unusual as a paper greeting card. Blanks come pre-assembled, so a touch of embroidery is all that's needed to turn a blank into an embellished treasure.

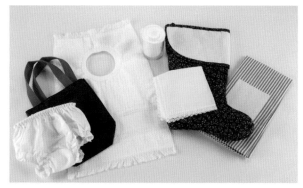

Credit: Embroider This!, Charles Craft

Within these pages, you'll find suggestions for placing embroidery designs on blanks. There is a list of online blank sellers, and ideas for finding blanks in brick-and-mortar retailers close to home. There are even a few thread and stabilizer guidelines; but if you are looking for detailed information on basic embroidery techniques, please refer to other sources as well.

You'll also find a baker's dozen projects on the enclosed CD-ROM, and a collection of embroidery designs to use for embellishing those and other embroidered delights. The projects were chosen to provide instructions for stitching on a variety of blank materials and constructions. They are focused on embroidery, not sewing.

The embroidery designs were created especially for this book by the author and three amazing digitizers: Evy Hawkins of A Bit of Stitch, Shelly Smola of My Fair Lady Designs, and Sherry Titzer of A Time to Stitch. These exclusive motifs are featured on samples throughout the book and are occasionally supplemented by other, commercially available designs.

So gather your embroidery supplies and fill in some blanks of your own!

Contents

The Bare Necessities

The most basic tools for machine embroidery – beyond the machine and motifs – are threads and stabilizers. Here are some quick and simple guidelines to consider as you embroider blanks. For more in-depth information, consult "Machine Embroidery with Confidence" by Nancy Zieman or the "Embroidery Machine Essentials" series by Jeanine Twigg and other embroidery experts.

THREADS

Machine embroidery threads are usually 40-weight rayon or polyester. These default threads are the ones digitizers have in mind, unless they specify something different for a particular design. Both rayon and polyester threads are available in many brands and come in a dazzling range of colors.

Embroiderers prize rayon threads for their silk-like sheen and the especially vibrant colors possible with this synthetic. Polyester threads are increasingly available in wide color ranges, and they have the advantage of greater colorfastness. Choose polyester threads for embroidering any blanks that will be exposed to heavy use and care, such as towels or garments for babies and children.

Occasionally a design will benefit from using a slightly heavier, 30-weight thread. The larger size fills in a design more completely, which can be a plus when the design and background are high contrast. An example is stitching a snowman on black fabric.

As more people join the home embroidery trend, thread choices have increased to include a variety of specialty threads. Look for cotton embroidery threads in 50-, 30- and even 12-weight to mimic a hand-stitched appearance or create heirloom lace embroideries. Wool blend threads used with specially digitized motifs look like crewel embroidery or create fuzzy designs with great tactile appeal. There are even threads that glow in the dark or change color in sunlight!

100
50
40
30
12

STABILIZERS

It's not overstating the case to say that stabilizers are crucial to all machine embroidery. It can be difficult to choose the best stabilizer for a particular job, and testing first is always recommended.

Here are general guidelines to consider:

Tear-away stabilizers are ideal for embroidering on stable fabrics, usually woven. They support the fabric and help prevent distortion during embroidery, but their support wanes during use and care.

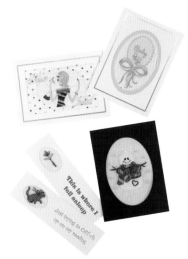

Cut-away stabilizers remain behind the embroidery permanently to provide continued support. They are essential when stitching on knits or unstable fabrics, and can also improve stitch quality on textured fabrics by providing a smooth underlayer for the stitches.

Adhesive stabilizers come in several varieties: iron-on, water-activated and self-adhesive (also called paper-release) in tear-away, cut-away, and water-soluble forms. Any adhesive stabilizer provides additional steadiness for embroidering on knits by locking in the fabric structure so it doesn't stretch during hooping and embroidery.

Credit: P.G.S. Specialties

Temporary adhesive spray can be used to render most stabilizers adhesive. Always protect your surroundings from over-spray by putting the hooped stabilizer in a box or garbage can before spraying. Use a light touch; too much spray adhesive will gum the needle and can lead to mechanical problems.

Adhesive stabilizers are also used to embroider items without hooping. By positioning the stabilizer alone in the hoop and activating or exposing its adhesive surface, an operator can position small items for embroidery or stitch on fabrics that would be damaged by the hoop's pressure.

When an adhesive stabilizer is used as a hooping aid, it's often beneficial to add an additional layer of stabilizer (tear-away or cut-away) to support the embroidery stitches. This is especially true when a design is very large or densely filled.

Soluble stabilizers are temporary notions that can be completely removed with the application of water or heat after embroidery. Like tear-away stabilizers, their support disappears with the stabilizer, but soluble stabilizers are invaluable for fine embroidery on sheer fabrics and when creating machine embroidered lace and other free-standing embroideries. Spray starch can also be used as a soluble stabilizer when only minimal support is required.

Toppers are a special category of stabilizers. They sit on top of the fabric and are covered only by the embroidery stitches. Toppers are used to prevent background colors from showing through embroidered motifs, and to control fabric nap. Unlike soluble stabilizers (which can be used as temporary toppers), vinyl

Credit: Embroider This!; Anita Goodesign

toppers remain on the fabric permanently and continue to function throughout the life of the project. Compressed foam is also a kind of topper, and is used to raise stitches above the background for a puffed effect.

ACCESSORIES

In addition to a machine and hoop, designs, stabilizers and thread, the following tools and notions will make embroidery a simpler process.

Machine embroidery needles in size 75/11 or 90/14 are appropriate for almost all thread types and embroidery tasks. Have a few additional needles on hand, such as topstitching needles for larger threads and jeans or micro-point needles for tricky outlines and fine fabrics.

Be sure you have good scissors dedicated to use on fabric. Keep a pair of thread snips near the machine, and have a pair of small, sharp scissors for trimming appliqué shapes. In addition, have a pair of scissors for cutting paper and template materials.

Rulers are a must for positioning monograms and motifs on blanks. A ruler marked both horizontally and vertically with a grid of lines is useful for squaring up placements. If your machine gives design sizes in metric increments, consider purchasing a metric ruler to avoid converting measurements between systems.

Credit: "Designs in Machine Embroidery," Embroidery Arts

Many specialty rulers and placement kits are available to aid embroiderers. These are particularly useful if you embroider the same kind of blanks often, and can make the repetitive task much simpler.

Marking tools can be chalk, pencil or soluble ink. All are useful, but always test before using to be sure the marks can be removed from a specific blank. Also remember that some marks are heat set, making them difficult or impossible to remove after an item has been ironed.

Blank Basics

What comes to mind first when looking for embroidery blanks are textile items: towels, t-shirts, and other household linens and wearing apparel.

For the most part, these fabric items consist of a single fabric layer, and they fit easily into the embroidery hoop.

Credit: The Sewphisticated Stitcher; "Designs in Machine Embroidery"

Other blanks are more unusual items created specifically for embroiderers and crafters. They are made with ingenious features that allow them to open up for embroidery; for example, terry slippers with a hook-and-loop tape fastener that separates the upper from the sole, or coasters with space to insert embroidered fabric.

Still other blanks may never have been intended for embroidery at all, but with the proper strategies in mind they can be adorned with stitched patches or embroidered covers. Most suppliers in the Resources section are Internet-based, because that marketplace is accessible to almost everyone. However, blanks to be embroidered need not come from distant sources. You will find many items to embroider in your own hometown…or even in your own home! Look in your closet for gently aged linens that can be freshened with embroidery. Outgrown articles of clothing make wonderful practice pieces for trying new embroidery techniques.

Check local discount and department stores for blank items: t-shirts and sweatshirts, jeans and jackets, towels, sheets, and other household linens. Hobby and fabric stores are great resources for blanks, too, as well as for fabric that can be embroidered separately and attached to "unembroiderable" blanks.

Credit: Charles Craft

A visit to needlework shops reveals a treasure trove of blanks intended for hand embroidery, but easily adapted to machine work. Look for afghans, bibs, towels with flat fabric inserts, doilies, tote bags, and lengths of Aida-cloth ribbon. Many hand needlework blanks are based on Aida cloth, a coarse fabric with a very regular weave. It's a perfect surface for both machine and hand cross-stitch, but can be used for other machine stitchery, too.

Flea markets, secondhand shops, and deep discount stores are great sources for blanks, too, but remember to shop with a discerning eye. Small stains and imperfections may be covered with embroidery to create wonderful new items, but cheaply made blanks aren't a good investment. Your embroidered creations deserve the good beginning of a well-made blank.

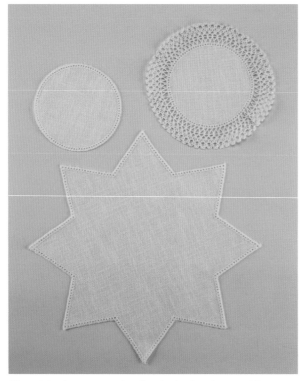

These blanks come with a finished edge designed for attaching hand-crocheted edging lace, but it's suitable for machine-embroidered lace, too.
Credit: Zweigart; Criswell Embroidery & Design

Prewashing blank items is usually a good practice. It both eliminates the threat of shrinkage and removes surface treatments that can affect stitch quality. Prewashing is especially important if the blank is a dark color that may bleed when wet and when water-soluble stabilizer will be used for embroidery. However, be sure the blank is made from a washable fiber and is a washable construction.

Launder the blank item according to the manufacturer's instructions; when in doubt, hand wash carefully in lukewarm water and line dry. Press the blank to remove wrinkles and creases before embroidering.

If an item cannot be washed – for example, a tote with an inner cardboard base – stay away from water-soluble stabilizers and marking tools that must be removed with water. In other cases, you may choose to skip prewashing because the finished project will not be washed.

In any event, it's a thoughtful and smart idea to include a care label or card with embroidered blanks given as gifts.

Starting Simple

The easiest and most common blanks for embroidery consist of a single fabric layer. They may be plain weave fabrics, as in handkerchiefs, linen towels and sheets, or terry cloth and other textured fabrics. The embroidery is often a monogram or name, either with additional embroidery motifs or without.

Credit: Embroider This!, Wimpole Street; Embroidery Arts

WHERE

Many embroiderers wonder exactly where on a particular blank the embroidery should be located. The question arises especially when a monogram or other personalization is being stitched.

"Correct" design placements are the product of both common sense and tradition. Common sense dictates that a motif should be positioned so it is right side up in use; that's not as straightforward as it sounds when the blank in question is a cuffed sock or a bed sheet that will be turned back when the bed is made. In other cases, the placement of a monogram may have no basis other than "It's always been done that way." Design placement is usually stated as a measurement from the blank's edge to the center of the embroidery, so the motif size is also a factor in determining placement.

Special tools are available to assist embroiderers in positioning motifs on many common blanks such as towels, napkins and shirts. These tools incorporate transparent templates and centering rulers as well as printed guides that offer instructions and placement ideas.

Ultimately, the placement decision is the embroiderer's. If a set of napkins is given with special napkin rings, the motif may be most attractively placed on the diagonal in one corner; but if the napkins will be folded in the table setting, a placement parallel to one side may be more appropriate.

Here are some basic guidelines for common embroidery placements to use as a starting point for stitching on blanks.

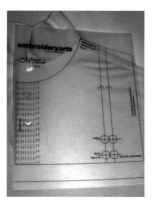

Credit: Embroidery Arts

SHEETS AND PILLOWCASES

- Above the hem placement:
- Sheets: Bottom of motif ½" above the hem. The bottom of the design is toward the hem so the motif is right side up when the sheet is folded back.
- Pillowcases: Bottom of motif ¼" above the hem.

On the hem/band placement: Select a design that is at least 1" shorter than the band's width and stitch it in the center (horizontally and vertically) of the band. For pillowcases, center the design on one side so it will fall to the outside of the bed when in use.

TOWELS

Credit: Embroidery Arts

- ◆ Bath towel with border: Bottom of motif 1½" above border.
- ◆ Bath towel without border: Bottom of motif 5" from bottom of towel.
- ◆ Hand towel with border: Bottom of motif 1" above border.
- ◆ Hand towel without border: Bottom of motif 3½" from bottom of towel.
- ◆ Washcloth with border: Bottom of motif 1" above border.
- ◆ Washcloth without border: Bottom of motif 1½" above hem or diagonally across one corner.
- ◆ Fingertip towels: Bottom of motif 2" above hem or 1" above border.

SHIRTS

- ◆ Left chest placement: 6" - 7½" from shoulder seam and about 1½" to the right from the neckline/shoulder intersection to embroidery center point. The best position varies with size and gender.
- ◆ Cuff: Center a small monogram on the left cuff with the letters' lower edge ¼" above the topstitching.
- ◆ T-shirt or sweatshirt: Center the design with its top edge 2½" below the neckline seam for adult sizes, 1" - 1½" for toddlers' shirts.

SHORTS

- ◆ Mark the center front of the left leg. Find a point halfway between the mark and the side seam.
- ◆ Position the motif with its center on the second mark and its lower edge ½" above the shorts' lower edge.

TIES

- ◆ Center the motif 2½" above the tie point.
- ◆ If worn with a vest, the design can be moved up to a point 9" to 11" above the point.

BAGS, TOTES AND PURSES

- ◆ Center the design 4" from the top edge, centered between straps.
- ◆ Vary placement with motif and bag size.

HOW

If the blank is large enough, embellishing it is a simple process of stabilizing, hooping and stitching. Small blanks or embroidery placements near finished edges call for a slightly different strategy.

One option is to hoop a piece of adhesive stabilizer. Either remove its protective paper to expose the adhesive surface or mist it with water to activate the adhesive, and attach the blank to the sticky surface.

Another strategy is to augment the blank's edges to make them large enough for hooping. Baste strips of stabilizer or scrap fabric to the blank's edges with needle and thread or temporarily fuse strips of stabilizer to the project's edges. Keep the basting stitches and added fabric outside the embroidery area, and remove the additions completely when the stitching is finished.

With single layer blanks, it's important to keep the wrong side tidy. Choose a removable stabilizer if possible, and use bobbin thread that matches the blank.

See the enclosed CD-ROM for complete instructions to make this embroidered towel and learn about embroidery on single-layer blanks.
Credit: Martha Pullen Company

LINEN TOWEL IDEAS

- ◆ Linen towels are a great base for heirloom motifs and designs that incorporate wing needle stitches.

- ◆ When stitching a multi-colored design, choose a single thread color for the bobbin that will make an attractive monochromatic pattern on the towel's wrong side.

- ◆ A densely filled embroidery motif may need a layer of tear-away stabilizer in addition to the water-soluble. Choose a design that will not add too much weight to the towel or cause the linen to buckle.

- ◆ Substitute textured kitchen towels for the pristine linen. A permanent vinyl topper under the embroidery counteracts the textured fabric and keeps all the embroidery stitches on the surface, while a cut-away stabilizer works the same way beneath the towel.

HANDKERCHIEF IDEAS

Handkerchiefs' popularity comes and goes, but they are always in style as a token gift. Women's hankies, plain hemmed or trimmed in lace, can be embroidered with a swirling monogram or colorful embroidery motif. For men, choose a simple

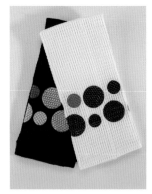

For these towels, the topper color matches the fabric rather than the thread color. The contrast emphasizes the texture of the embroidery stitches.

Handkerchief bunny.
Credit: McCalls Creates; Brother

monogram of one to three letters to create a functional accessory or a stylish jacket pocket adornment.

Fine linen or cotton handkerchiefs are a wonderful surface for experimenting with wing needle embroidery. A wing needle is designed with projections (wings) on either side of its shank to open a hole between fabric threads. Used in combination with embroidery designs created for wing needle work, it mimics the appearance of time-consuming pulled thread embroidery done by hand.

Your embroidered handkerchief need not simply take the place of paper tissues in your pocket. Hankies make a great start for many simple projects.

- ◆ Embroider all four corners of a handkerchief and lay it diagonally across the top of a purchased pillow. Tack the corners to the pillow top for a beautiful decorative accent.
- ◆ Use handkerchiefs as the basis for stuffed animals and dolls. Take advantage of embroidered corners and pre-hemmed edges as you cut the project pieces.
- ◆ Use embroidered handkerchiefs as quilt blocks or embellishments in a crazy quilt.
- ◆ Convert a flat handkerchief into a baby bonnet with a few stitches and a bit of ribbon. When the baby is grown and marries, release the stitches for a "something old" handkerchief to be carried by the bride.

TEXTURED FABRICS: AIDA AND WAFFLE WEAVE

Aida cloth is familiar to hand embroidery enthusiasts as an ideal fabric for counted cross-stitch. Its consistently even weave is created by groups of threads and forms visible holes between fibers. Waffle weave uses its unique construction to create a fabric with well-defined rectangular ridges that rise above a solidly filled background.

For more about embroidering with a wing needle, see "Machine Embroidery Wild & Wacky."
Credit: Wimpole Street; Criswell Embroidery & Design

Machine embroiderers sometimes use Aida cloth and blanks in conjunction with machine cross-stitch motifs to create projects that mimic hand needlework almost perfectly. For this technique, precise hooping and design placement combine to ensure the needle drops into the fabric spaces and forms stitches over the yarns' intersections. (For more on machine cross stitch, see "Machine Embroidery Wild & Wacky.")

Credit: Charles Craft

Of course, machine cross-stitch motifs can be stitched on other fabrics, too, even those without an even weave. What's less obvious is Aida's suitability for machine embroidered designs of other types.

To embroider successfully on Aida cloth or a waffle weave, their highly textured surfaces must be neutralized to mimic embroidery on flat fabric. Use a medium- or heavyweight cut-away stabilizer to support the stitches evenly no matter where they fall on the Aida weave. It may also be beneficial to cover the textured fabric with a topper to hold the stitches above the surface, especially if the design incorporates satin stitches. Temporary or permanent toppers will work. Appliqué motifs work as toppers, too, if the embroidery stitches fall atop the appliqué fabric.

✓ *Tip*

Definitely pre-wash Aida blanks when using a water-soluble stabilizer or if the project will be washed, since Aida is susceptible to shrinkage.

Complete instructions for this embroidered baby blanket can be found on the enclosed CD-ROM. It's a good introduction to embroidery on textured blanks, and includes a technique for tidying the blanket's wrong side.
Credit: Charles Craft

Aprons are another great single-layer blank.
Credit: Embroider This!, My Embroidery Haven

MAKE SOMETHING OF IT

Linen towels and handkerchiefs are the tip of the single-layer blank iceberg. Any single-layer item stitched from a stable woven fabric can be embellished with the techniques outlined above. Their woven construction renders them durable and easy to embroider for quick but lovely gifts and decorations.

Credit: Brother

Look for linen table runners, doilies, coasters and tablecloths to embellish. Some feature drawn-thread embellishment that divides the blank into sections just the right size for embroidered motifs. Stitch a design in every section, or pick just a few for embellishment.

See the enclosed CD-ROM for instructions to create this ring bearer's pillow.
Credit: All About Blanks

SHAPING UP

Cocktail napkins come in rectangles and other shapes. Use a pair of square napkins to create an ornament or doorknob decoration. Sew them together with wrong sides facing, stuff, and add a simple ribbon hanger.

A place mat becomes a purse with a few simple stitches along the sides and an added handle of ribbon, fabric, plastic or wood. Position the embroidery motif with the end use in mind.

Turn a table runner into a simple lingerie bag. Fold just over one third of the runner length up, wrong sides together, and stitch the sides. The other end becomes a flap to close the lingerie keeper.

Credit: Embroider This!

Rotate the Deco Frame motif 45 degrees and stitch it in splashy colors to match the place mat trim. Compare this design to the golf towels on page 27 to see what a difference color can make.

Insert a pillow form into the lingerie keeper and close the top edge to make an envelope pillow from the table runner. If the runner is very long (72" x 14" is a good size), cut it in half and make two pillows from a single runner.

Credit: Wimpole Street

Tees and Sweats

T-shirts are arguably the most often embroidered blanks. They are an inexpensive canvas for decorative work, and almost everyone from babies to grandparents wears them at some time or another.

But embroidery on a t-shirt or sweatshirt need not be simply a single motif stitched dead center or on the left upper chest. Read on for some different placement ideas and tips on making embroidery on knits look its best.

THE INVISIBLE SUPPORT

Stabilizer is the unseen champion of embroidery on knit fabrics. It serves two important functions: counteracting the fabric stretch as the embroidery design is stitched, and supporting the thread and stitches over time as the shirt is worn and washed.

Choose an iron-on or adhesive stabilizer to immobilize the knit structure during embroidery. This stabilizer can be attached to the knit before hooping the two layers as one, or it can be hooped separately with the shirt attached to its adhesive surface. For extra stability, use the machine's basting function to stitch the layers together temporarily around the hoop perimeter. (For more, see page 22.)

Select a cut-away stabilizer to support the motif after embroidery. This may be the same stabilizer as the iron-on or adhesive mentioned above, or a separate layer slipped ("floated") under the hoop. Use a heavyweight cut-away for sweatshirts or very dense motifs, and a lightweight cut-away mesh for tees.

LOCATION, LOCATION, LOCATION

As an alternative to the ordinary plop-and-drop placement of a single embroidery motif, consider these ideas for stitching on tees and sweats.

Credit: Brother

- Stitch a specially digitized neckline motif around the shirt's neckband, or group a series of motifs around the neck from shoulder to shoulder.

- Group several motifs of different sizes and shapes into an interesting puzzle layout. Use customizing software and a large hoop, or print full-size templates, and use them to play with the design arrangement. Take a quick digital snapshot of the template arrangement as a guide to use when embroidering, and mark the center point and top edge of each motif on the shirt before removing the templates.

Credit: OESD

◆ Stitch several motifs in a line across the shirt. The motifs can be the same or different. While a line across the upper chest is the most traditional, consider stitching a vertical line from shoulder to hem instead, or a band of motifs just above the shirt hem. If the band consists of repeats of a single motif, stitch just one in a different color or as a mirror image of the others for a whimsical accent.

Credit: Embroidery Arts

The design and instructions for this twin set are included on the CD-ROM at the back of the book. Use this project as a starting point for experimenting with unusual design placements on t-shirts.

Denim Shirts and Jeans

Casual denim shirts probably run a close second to tees as the favorite canvas for home embroiderers, and embroidered jeans are a fashion must today. Like t-shirts, they become extraordinary with a little imagination in placing embroidery designs.

Credit: Sue Box

- Pockets are like frames for embroidery designs. Choose a motif that fits within the pocket area, or select a pocket topper motif that creates the illusion it's sprouting from inside the pocket. For a whimsical touch, position an embroidery design as if it is dangling from the pocket point.

- Look for short, narrow motifs to place on the button placket between buttonholes. Stitch designs between the buttons instead for a peek-a-boo effect.

- Stitch a tiny motif at one collar point. Mirror the design and stitch it on the opposite collar point. For variety, embroider a design on the collar at the center back instead, or embroider the collar band rather than the collar itself for a design that's visible when the collar is turned up.

- So-called "windowpane" shirts are constructed with strips of fabric dividing the shirt fronts into perfectly sized embroidery locations. Use one to showcase a favorite set of coordinating motifs, or fill only a few windows with embroidery to create a faux check or to suggest a yoke.

Credit: Embroidery Library

Credit: Brother

- Yokes on shirts and pants are a great canvas for embroidery. Arrange several motifs to fill the yoke area. Scatter a coordinating motif or two elsewhere on the shirt for an overall design.

- Position a motif at the center back, between the shoulders.

- Embellish the cuffs with segments of a border motif or with a series of small designs.

- Stitch a large motif or border along the side seam of your favorite jeans, or arrange the motif to spiral around one leg.

- Embroider a gently curved design at the jeans front pocket opening.

- Decorate a jeans hem with a wide or narrow border motif.

Credit: Embroidables

Strategic Maneuvers

Unlike t-shirts, denim shirts are tailored with collars, plackets, cuffs and pockets, each of which is both an embroidery opportunity and a roadblock to hooping. While a traditional left-chest, over-the-pocket placement for a monogram or small logo is easily stabilized with tear-away or adhesive stabilizer, working with small areas and double layers calls for some different strategies.

POCKETS

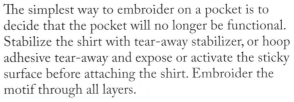

The simplest way to embroider on a pocket is to decide that the pocket will no longer be functional. Stabilize the shirt with tear-away stabilizer, or hoop adhesive tear-away and expose or activate the sticky surface before attaching the shirt. Embroider the motif through all layers.

To maintain the pocket's functionality, you might embroider a pocket topper instead. Use a full-size template to position the embroidery design so its lower edge is slightly below the top of the pocket and mark the embroidery position. Hoop as directed above. Roll the pocket upper edge down and away from the embroidery area and pin or tape to hold it outside the stitching area. Embroider the motif at the marked placement.

The pocket can also be removed completely from the garment for embroidery. Use a seam ripper to take out the stitches holding the pocket in place. Hoop adhesive stabilizer and attach the pocket to it for embroidery. Replace the pocket on the shirt when embroidery is complete, and use matching thread to reattach the pocket. If matching thread isn't available, pick a contrasting color that coordinates with the embroidery and make the pocket topstitching a design feature, too.

One other pocket strategy is especially useful when the pocket's upper edge is reinforced with a heavy bartack or metal rivet. In that case, remove the stitches holding the pocket in place below the

With careful planning, a large pocket can be attached to adhesive stabilizer and embroidered through only one fabric thickness. Choose a relatively small design, fold the main part of the blank out of the way, and reposition the blank as needed so the area under the needle is always flat and free of wrinkles.
Credit: The Sewphisticated Stitcher

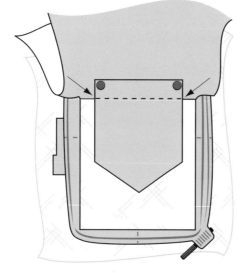

Release the stitches below the arrows and attach the pocket to hooped stabilizer.

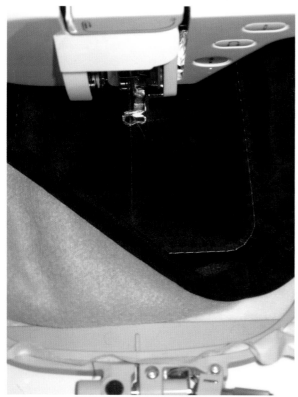

Credit: The Sewphisticated Stitcher

reinforcements, but leave the pocket attached at the upper edge. Fold the shirt out of the way and attach the pocket to adhesive stabilizer for embroidery. After stitching the motif, reattach the pocket to the shirt below the reinforcements.

PLACKETS, CUFFS AND COLLARS

These three design features have one thing in common: the embroidery decorating them will be placed very near an edge. In combination with the thickness of seams in those areas, that means ordinary hooping methods won't work for stitching on these little pieces.

Instead, turn to adhesive stabilizer. Place a tear-away or water-soluble adhesive stabilizer in the hoop and attach the placket, cuff or collar to it.

If the garment area is thick or has a tendency to shift, or if the bulk of the garment away from the hoop tugs the embroidery area loose, stabilize it further by basting the garment to the stabilizer. Some machines provide basting stitch patterns for this function. If yours does not, try one of these options instead:

- ◆ Use digitizing software to create a square, circle or rectangle of long running stitches that's larger than the embroidery design. Stitch this pattern first to baste the garment to the stabilizer.

- ◆ Some machines have frame patterns built in. A running-stitch frame can be used for basting.

- ◆ Straight pins placed well outside the embroidery area can be used to attach the garment to the stabilizer.

- ◆ Masking tape, double-sided tape or regular office tape can be used to secure the garment to the stabilizer outside the embroidery area.

- ◆ Caution: Some fabrics retain needle holes and should not be basted. Vinyl is one example. Other materials such as velvet may be bruised or crushed by basting stitches. Using a fine needle and silk thread minimizes the damage. Always test first on a fabric sample or inconspicuous area of the blank to be sure the basting can be easily removed.

In selecting the specific stabilizer to use, consider whether the embroidery wrong side will be visible when the garment is worn. For example, a cuff or collar could be turned back, revealing the bobbin threads. In those cases choose a water-soluble adhesive stabilizer that will disappear completely from the finished work. The double thickness of the shirt will provide the continued support the embroidery needs.

NARROW AREAS

Pant legs, sleeves and even small-size garments may be too narrow to hoop while keeping other parts of the garment out of the needle's path. Try these strategies for hooping narrow areas:

- ◆ Turn the project inside out. Fuse stabilizer to the wrong side of the embroidery area. While the garment is wrong side out, place the outer hoop on the work surface with the garment on top. Slide the inner hoop inside the garment and clamp the halves of the hoop together. Attach the hoop to the machine and arrange the garment into a sort of tunnel around the needle bar. Stay with the machine as it embroiders to keep the garment away from the needle.

- ◆ Open a seam in the area opposite the embroidery position. For example, open the inseam of a pair of jeans or the underarm seam of a sleeve. This allows the garment to be positioned flat for hooping or attached to hooped adhesive stabilizer.

- ◆ If the garment includes decorative seams, such as the flat felled seams on jeans, or a special hem that would be hard to restitch, leave those features intact. Most areas of a sleeve or pant leg can be accessed for embroidery by opening the inseam, side or underarm seam only above the hem or cuff.

INSIDE OUT INSIGHTS

Turning the project inside out makes embroidery possible on many blanks: tubes such as sleeves and socks, pant legs, and pillow covers. Stretchy fabric can make positioning the blank easier, but it's not essential for the technique. Just

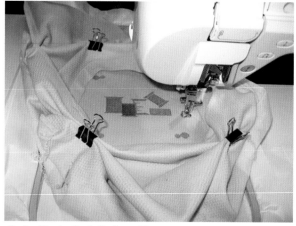

Credit: Charles Craft; Sudberry House

remember that only the portion of the blank where the needle is entering the fabric has to be exposed at a given moment.

Mark the embroidery location while the blank is still right side out. Slide the outer hoop into the blank and lay the inner hoop on top of the location to hoop the stabilized blank directly, or turn the blank inside out and affix the design area to hooped adhesive stabilizer.

Arrange the other portions of the inside-out blank around the presser foot. Binder clips may be useful to hold the fabric out of the way, but they aren't foolproof and can even create problems if they bump into the needle bar or presser foot. Always stay with the machine as it stitches, and use hands placed well away from the needle to ensure the excess fabric isn't caught in the embroidery stitches.

Pre-made pillow covers are constructed with overlapping panels on the back. By turning the pillow wrong side out and working through the back opening, it may be possible to embroider the pillow without opening a single seam. Choose a small design placed in the center of the pillow for easiest embroidery. Buttons, bows or decorative machine stitches around the small motif extend it visually to fill the pillow space.

The central area of an inside-out blank is always the easiest portion to embroider. Circular motifs and diamonds (squares placed on point), even if they fill much of the pillow, work well on pre-made pillow covers because they don't extend into the hard-to-embroider corners.

Credit: Charles Craft

Terrific Terry

Credit: *The Sewphisticated Stitcher*

Is terry cloth terrific or terrible? As popular as terry towels are with embroiderers, there are special considerations to keep the embroidery looking great as the towels are used and laundered.

What makes terry cloth unique – its loopy texture – is also what makes terry a challenge for embroiderers. To create a design that looks great and wears well, the nap must be controlled during embroidery and afterward. It's much like the need to control a t-shirt's stretch and provide continuing support for the stitches.

In addition, terry toweling can be very bulky, which presents its own hooping challenges. One solution is to loosen the hoop as much as possible before inserting the towel and stabilizer, then tightening the outer hoop to fit. Even then the hoop may not grip the towel securely, and the vibration created by the machine can cause the inner hoop to pop free, releasing the towel and ruining the embroidery.

Instead, many embroiderers hoop adhesive stabilizer and attach the terry towel to the stabilizer without hooping. In choosing the best stabilizer, balance its ability to hold the towel securely with the need to release the towel after stitching without pulling the terry loops. A water-activated stabilizer can be re-moistened to loosen the adhesive bond, and an adhesive water-soluble stabilizer will dissolve without pulling the terry loops, so both are excellent choices.

Basting the towel to the hooped stabilizer also helps ensure a secure hold during embroidery. Large towels in particular are weighty enough to cause design distortions if the towel outside the hoop slips off the machine table or shifts while the machine is running, and basting helps counteract that problem.

When choosing motifs for terry embroidery, select those with fill or satin stitches bold enough to flatten the nap. Running stitch motifs and designs with small details tend to become lost in the terry surface.

An easy way to combat the tendency toward disappearing designs on terry is to use a topper to keep the stitches on top of the nap. Toppers come in several forms, and are either temporary or permanent. The simplest way to use a topper is to hoop the towel sandwiched between stabilizer and a water-soluble film topper. The water-soluble film flattens the terry loops so the stitches form on top of a relatively smooth, flat surface.

But it's important to remember that, as the towel is used and laundered, temporary toppers dissolve completely. Once their restraining presence is removed,

the embroidery design threads will shift back and forth and eventually the terry loops will pop up between the stitches.

Permanent toppers are the solution. A permanent topper might be a closely spaced grid of understitching behind the decorative motif or a layer of organza that matches the towel color. Another option is permanent vinyl topping, available in many colors, or an all-purpose clear type. The vinyl is laid on the hooped towel before stitching begins and becomes a permanent barrier between the terry loops and embroidery stitches. Vinyl toppers are also useful for improving the appearance of light-colored stitches against a dark background when the topper matches the thread color. The vinyl topper tears easily after perforation by the needle. Remove the excess before stitching the design outline for a tidy finish.

Yet another permanent topper is appliquéd fabric. It differs from the other toppers in being a visible part of the embellishment. Choose an embroidery design that includes areas of appliqué to decorate your towel, or create an appliqué patch in a simple geometric shape to fit behind the embroidered motif. Appliqués create a smooth embroidery surface so that even fine details are visible. For a truly tidy wrong side, stitch the main motif on the appliqué fabric before attaching the appliqué to the towel. (For more on this idea, see the Miss Priss Cosmetic Case instructions on the enclosed CD-ROM.)

Appliquéd fabric makes an excellent permanent topper, and embroidering on the fabric before attaching it to the towel yields a tidy back, too.

A simple change of color and font takes this design from masculine to feminine. See the place mat purse on page 16 for another take on this versatile motif, and look to the enclosed CD-ROM for instructions on creating the golf towel with appliquéd fabric as a topper.
Credit: The Sewphisticated Stitcher

TOWEL TOUCHES

Monograms are the traditional embellishment for towels, buy why stop there?

◆ Stitch a matching towel and washcloth for a child. Add an appliqué motif that doubles as a pocket for the washcloth, or stitch a buttonhole on the washcloth and a novelty button on the towel.

◆ Don't restrict towel thoughts to the bathroom. Some kitchen towels are terry, too, and beach towels make a wonderful large canvas for beach- and pool-themed motifs.

◆ With a little ingenuity, towels can be used as the building blocks for a new mother's bath apron, a hooded baby towel, a beach tote, a pool chair cushion, and many other simple projects.

◆ Apply a bit of imagination to the traditional "His" and "Hers" set and stitch a group of towels to tickle any fancy.

◆ Unsure about names for a newly married couple? Create a unique gift without monogramming by stitching a set of fingertip towels for occasions throughout the year. Christmas, Easter, Chanukah, Halloween, Thanksgiving, and New Year's Day are all possibilities. Definitely include Valentine's Day, and a wedding anniversary towel personalized with the couple's date.

Credit: Embroidery Library

Fabulous Fleece

The design and instructions for making this afghan are on the enclosed CD-ROM. It's a great project for experimenting with embroidery and appliqué on fleece.

Fleece is one of the most popular fabrics today. It's soft, warm and easy to care for. Fleece comes in a wide range of colors and prints, in light weights for transitional seasons and warm climates and in heavy constructions for combating cold weather.

To embroider on fleece, think of it as a combination of t-shirt's stretch and terry's nap. The stabilizer used for fleece embroidery needs to control the stretch during embroidery. An additional topper may be necessary to flatten the fleece nap for embroidery of lasting quality. Appliqué motifs are wonderful on fleece fabrics, with the appliqué shapes cut from either woven fabric or other colors of fleece.

For a different appearance, try texturizing fleece with embroidery stitches. Stitch quilting motifs, appliqué outlines (without the fabric appliqué) and simple openwork motifs on fleece with matching thread. As the stitches compress the fleece nap, an embossed appearance results, where the texture is more evident than the embroidery details. (See photo above.)

If the project wrong side will be visible – for example, when stitching on a fleece afghan – choose a technique that will minimize the visibility of bobbin threads. This is also important on baby blankets that will come into contact with an infant's tender skin, because embroidery bobbin thread can be surprisingly scratchy and irritating.

Here are some strategies for beautiful backs:

- ◆ Use a bobbin thread color that matches the project. It will blend into the fabric on the wrong side. If the colored thread is not the same weight and type as the usual bobbin thread, test stitch first to be sure of a successful result.

- ◆ Change bobbin thread colors every time the needle thread changes for a reversible motif.

- ◆ Surround the motif with an appliquéd frame motif such as an oval or square. Stitch the frame shape last, and apply the appliqué to the project wrong side, where it will cover the motif's bobbin threads.

- ◆ Use the same thread in needle and bobbin when attaching a fleece appliqué to a fleece blank. Cut away the blank inside the appliqué placement stitches to reveal the appliquéd fleece shape on both sides.

- ◆ Embroider motifs on an afghan blank with regular bobbin thread and embroidery techniques. Cut a piece of coordinating fabric ½" larger all around than the afghan (without fringe). Press ½" to the wrong side on the coordinating fabric edges. Place the fabric on the embroidered afghan, wrong sides together, and edgestitch near the pressed edges through all layers. Topstitch the afghan and fabric together between the embroidered motifs to create an afghan/quilt with two finished sides.

Double Layers

Some blanks are constructed with two fabric layers, with or without batting or other fill in between. Examples are lined windbreakers and nylon-backed stadium blankets.

Credit: The Sewphisticated Stitcher

One approach to embroidering double-layer blanks is to open a seam in the lining and use one of the hooping strategies outlined on pages 21-24 to stitch on the outer layer only. This method yields a beautiful back, since the lining covers the bobbin side of the work, but sewing is required to reattach the lining after embroidery.

If the item is part of a large job order, the extra time can be a major additional expense. But for embroidery on fine apparel, or if the embroidery is to be placed on the garment lining, the time to partially remove and replace the lining is certainly justified.

Another option is to embroider through both layers of the blank as if it were a single thickness. For success, the layers must be rendered as much like a single layer as possible.

- First, pin through both layers around the embroidery design location to ensure that the layers are correctly matched. Try on the garment if possible to be sure it does not sag or bunch.

- Next, hoop the two layers together with stabilizer if possible. Where hooping presents problems, use an adhesive stabilizer and attach the blank to the hooped stabilizer, but remember that only the bottom layer of the blank is truly stabilized.

- To join the layers for embroidery and prevent the top layer from shifting, baste the layers around the hoop perimeter before beginning the embroidery. See page 22 for more about basting in the hoop.

- If the upper layer is napped or has a tendency to stretch, stabilize it with a water-soluble film stabilizer applied before the basting stitches.

Once the multi-layer blank is stabilized, embroider it as usual.

Smocking

Traditional smocking is a lovely technique of hand-worked stitches placed on a background of precisely even pleats. A variation, picture smocking, uses blocks of stitches to create filled embroidery motifs on the pleated ground.

Fabric for smocking is prepared by placing rows of equally spaced gathering stitches across the entire area to be smocked. This is accomplished by hand, using a grid of dots transferred to the fabric wrong side, or by passing the fabric through a pleating machine with multiple needles to make parallel rows of gathering stitches all at once.

Credit: Martha Pullen Company; Deb Yedziniak

Machine embroidery stitches can successfully mimic the look of hand smocking. In addition, machine embroidered motifs can be stitched on pleated fabric bands to give textural interest to a project or to accomplish fitting in garment sections.

Pre-smocked blanks have recently been introduced to the embroidery market. These blanks are completely assembled garments with rows of pleating in place and ready for embroidered embellishment. In addition, bands of pleated fabric can be ordered from blanks suppliers or at shops that specialize in heirloom sewing and smocking materials.

✓ Tip

If you are embroidering on pleated fabric that is not already stitched into a garment, the width of the pleating can be adjusted by moving the pleats closer together or farther apart before stabilizing and embroidering.

Although almost invisible, the rows of machine stitching hold the pleats in place across the entire area.
Credit: Martha Pullen Company

Picture smocking isn't just for hand embroiderers any-
more! See the enclosed CD-ROM for these designs and
instructions for machine embroidery on smocking pleats.
Credit: Martha Pullen Company

One concession must be made to prepare pleated items for machine embroidery. Hand smocking stitches cover all the pleats across the project width, keeping the pleats intact after the gathering threads are removed. Because the machine embroidered motif covers only part of the pleated area, other stitches must be used to keep the pleats intact.

This can be accomplished by hand using a technique called back smocking, in which simple rows of ordinary smocking stitches are worked in matching thread across the entire pleated area on the wrong side. Sewing parallel diagonal rows of machine stitches in matching thread will also secure the pleats. The rows of stitching will be visible on the project right side, but subtle enough to blend into the background and not interfere with the machine embroidered design.

Ageless Giving

Credit: Charles Craft; Vermillion Stitchery; Stephanie Corina Goddard. Photo courtesy of Charles Craft.

A monogram or name stitched on a towel or tote has tremendous appeal, and a personalized gift reveals special love and care on the part of the giver. With the variety of blanks beckoning embroiderers, it's easy to expand the gift repertoire. Vary the blank, the design, the monogram font or even the thread colors to adapt a gift for recipients of any age or gender.

FOR BABIES

Baby gifts are often made before the child is born. That means the baby's name and gender may be unknown when the gift is assembled. What's more, authorities caution against labeling clothing and accessories with a child's name to discourage the false familiarity of strangers.

Instead, opt for storybook motifs, cheerful animals and even bold geometric motifs. Use bright colors to stimulate the baby's senses and bring a smile to adults as well. Keep the designs small so they fit on baby garments, or opt for an afghan or décor item to provide a larger canvas.

The enclosed CD-ROM contains the designs and instructions for embroidering these designs on jersey knit baby bibs, but they are adaptable for terry and Aida cloth bibs, too.
Credit: Embroider This!

✓ *Tip*

Bobbin threads are scratchier than adults realize and can irritate a baby's delicate skin. A simple solution is to cover the wrong side of the completed embroidery with a soft, lightweight, fusible interfacing. Cut the interfacing slightly larger than the embroidery motif and round its corners. Use pinking shears for an edge that will blend into the project fabric and be invisible from the right side. Follow the manufacturer's instructions for a secure bond when fusing to ensure the project will endure use and care.

FOR CHILDREN

T-shirts embroidered with a favorite cartoon character are a staple in the embroiderer's repertoire, but many other blanks are ideal for children's gifts.

Stuffed animals may be difficult to embroider, but their clothes are not! Look for diminutive shirts, shorts, jackets and other clothing items that are sized to fit teddy bears and other animals or dolls. Most will be too small to hoop, but they are easily attached to hooped stabilizer for embroidering. Open snaps or hook-and-loop-tape fasteners to access the embroidery area, or use the inside-out hooping strategies mentioned on pages 23-24.

Towels can be both personal and educational. A specially embroidered bath set may encourage the youngest recipient to practice healthy habits.

Fabric or vinyl lunch boxes and bags with unique embroidered decorations are easy to identify in a group, and a child may be less likely to misplace or forget a special lunch carrier.

Wall hangings, fabric organizers for toys and shoes, growth charts and other décor items can be embroidered with colorful motifs that appeal to children. Decorative items are more gently used than clothing, so they may last longer… and they won't be outgrown as clothing will!

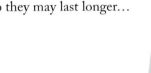

Credit: Embroider This!, Charles Craft; Anita Goodesign

Credit: The Sewphisticated Stitcher

✓ *Tip*

Teddy bears appeal to teens and adults, too. Bear clothing embellished with a team logo or mascot, or personalized with an athlete's name and number, can be a great fundraiser. One caution: many logos are trademarked, so be sure to check the legalities before creating items for sale.

FOR TEENS

Take inspiration from things every teenager uses. Consider items that are used at home, away from peer inspection; while a t-shirt lovingly stitched with the car of a boy's dreams my languish in the back of a drawer, a similarly embellished laundry bag will get plenty of use. Pillowcases are another item that can be personalized for boys or girls.

Organizers are another possibility. An armchair caddy can hold a remote control or knitting needles and yarn; embellish closet or wall organizers with words that indicate their use (Curling Iron - Brush - Hair Dryer, or Game Console - Games - Accessories). Other favorites: a monogrammed shaving kit, cosmetic bag, or a personalized gym bag.

Learn about creating embroidered appliqués as you stitch this fun-loving cosmetic case. Three versions of the design and complete instructions are on the enclosed CD-ROM.
Credit: All About Blanks

Credit: Walnut Hollow

Credit: ScrapSMART

FOR GUYS

Young or old, men enjoy embroidered gifts, too. Whether the idea is traditional monograms on handkerchiefs and cuffs or op-art embellishments on ties, there's a blank that's suited to the task.

If the man in question is a sports fan, consider stadium-friendly items with his name or initials. Afghans, seat covers, and drink holders are all possibilities. For an athletic man, personalize a gym bag or golf towel.

Armchair sports enthusiasts and tailgaters may enjoy witty words on a barbecue apron or an armchair caddy for their remote controls.

Other possibilities are desk accessories, from embroidered boxes to bookmarks, and masculine home décor. See page 37 for a clock project designed specifically to appeal to men and boys.

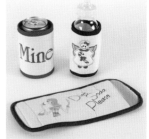

Stitch an insulated drink holder for the man on your list, or vary the motif to make it a feminine gift or a bottle warmer for baby!
Credit: Embroider This!; Embroidery Library

INSTANT IDEAS

Everyone has experienced the need for a thoughtful gift, worthy of the recipient, which must be ready and wrapped in no time. Here are some ideas to use when tomorrow isn't soon enough:

- Appliquéd motifs stitch in a fraction of the time required for filled designs of similar size.

- Look for designs created only with outlines. In addition to redwork and quilting motifs, this category includes artistic motifs that render their subject with a handful of satin stitch strokes.

- Chose designs with few color changes. Even a single color can create a beautifully shaded design.

- Monograms, names or humorous slogans have broad appeal. Dress up bare letters with a decorative frame or by embroidering a small motif on, near or in place of the letters; for example, "Beach Tote" with a colorful beach ball in place of the "O".

- Purchase one or two highly decorative fonts for fast, impressive monograms. A single large letter may be enough for a towel, tote or other gift.

- During sales, accumulate a stash of blanks to have on hand for late nights when those dreaded words are spoken: "By the way Mom, I have to have a gift for my teacher in the morning."

FOR THE PERSON WITH EVERYTHING

Blanks suppliers are nothing if not inventive, so their wares include an assortment of unusual gifts. Chances are there's something available that even the most gifted person has yet to receive. Here are a few examples:

Pet items
Credit: Crafter's Pride; In the Hoop Designs

Toilet paper holder
Credit: All About Blanks

Lotion dispenser
Credit: Crafter's Pride

Switch plate covers
Credit: Anita Goodesign

Tissue box cover
Credit: Crafter's Pride

Mouse pad
Credit: Embroider This!

How'd You Do It?

Yes, these foam can holders are embellished with embroidery! The secret is specially digitized motifs that perforate separate foam sheets, making the cutouts that are then glued in place.
Credit: Criswell Embroidery & Design

For real fun, expand the concept of blanks to include non-traditional, and even non-textile, items. In most cases, the techniques are easy and fast, but the WOW factor is enormous!

Embroidery is possible on a variety of surfaces, including paper, wood, pet screen and metal. Single layer blanks made from these materials are all candidates for embroidered embellishment.

Three-dimensional blanks can be embroidered, too. In most cases, the strategy for embellishing dimensional blanks utilizes blank fabric that is applied to the project with glue, fusing agents or other adhesives.

- ◆ Use glue to apply embroidered fabric to wood, plastic and other materials that will not warp when wet. Choose a glue that is appropriate for the base material. White craft glue and hot glue are two options, but consider permanent spray adhesives and pastes, too.

- ◆ Fusible webs and sprays work well for securing embroidered paper or fabric to flat surfaces that won't be damaged by heat. Cover the embroidery with a press cloth before applying the iron. Don't use fusing agents on plastic or foam.

- ◆ Other adhesives include dots and lines created for the scrapbooking market. Double-sided tape can be useful, too. Always read and follow the manufacturer's instructions.

Embroidery on paper is easy and sure to impress. Find the designs and instructions for these paper (and fabric) cards on the enclosed CD-ROM.
Credit: P. G. S. Specialties, Nature's Garden

Decorate gift bags, too. Turn large handmade paper bags inside out and embroider directly on them. For smaller bags, stitch a design on paper or fabric and apply as a patch with glue or fusible adhesive.
Credit: Nature's Garden

As an introduction to embellishing non-embroiderable blanks, create a lamp and shade to decorate any room. The adhesive is part of the blank itself; the designs and instructions are on the enclosed CD-ROM.
Credit: Wisconsin Lighting/Hollywood Lights

Learn to make flat, embroidered insertions to embellish clocks and other items with this project, found on the enclosed CD-ROM.

Credit: Walnut Hollow

TIMELY IDEAS

In addition to the embroidered clock face pictured above, there are other ways to stitch extraordinary timepieces:

◆ Create your own clock faces. Position the numerals 30 degrees apart.

◆ The central hole for the stem is the only essential feature of an embroidered clock face, so have some creative fun.

• Use a decorative font for the numerals.

• Replace some or all of the numerals with small embroidery designs.

• Choose a wreath design for the central area of the clock face or arrange designs to fit within the space between the stem and the numerals.

• Use editing software to delete stitches from a ⅜"-diameter area at the center of a filled motif to make an opening for the stem.

• Move the numerals toward the center and position a circle of designs or a decorative border around the outer edge of the clock face.

◆ Clock kits are available that feature precut but unfinished wood with a clear plastic cover to frame a special photograph. Replace the photo with embroidery for special personalization.

Vinyl accessories like these can be embellished with any embroidery, and it's easy to change the embroidered insert to suit a different mood or season.
Credit: ScrapSMART

These pillows required no sewing or glue. The secret is in the special pillow forms that hold embroidered fabric securely in place.
Credit: June Tailor; Embroidery Arts

INSERT HERE…AND THERE

The embroidered insert technique employed with the clock kit is useful for a variety of blanks. Choose a sturdy woven fabric that's easy to embroider, cotton broadcloth and weaver's cloth are good choices, with a weave that accepts most embroidery motifs and is tight enough to prevent severe fraying at the cut edges.

Cut-away stabilizer is sometimes used as the base for embroidered inserts. It is a good choice when the entire surface will be covered with embroidery, for example, in creating freestanding flower petals. Test first with the design and stabilizer chosen for the project to ensure a satisfactory finish without puckers.

Sometimes the insertion fabric needs to be stiffened to make placing it in the blank easier. Spray starch can be used as a stiffener, but it will yellow over time and is not the best choice for projects intended to last.

Another option is to glue or fuse the embroidered fabric to cardstock. Before trimming the embroidered fabric to size, back it with paper-backed fusible web. Remove the protective paper and lay the embroidery on a sheet of cardstock. Cover with a press cloth and fuse. Use the tip of the iron or a small craft iron to fuse right up to the embroidery stitches. Cut the paper-backed fabric to size and insert it into the blank.

Learn to make padded attachments for boxes, jars and tins with the instructions for these projects on the enclosed CD-ROM.

See boxes, jars and tins project on enclosed CD-ROM.

For an even simpler lid decoration, purchase ready-made jar-topper blanks.
Credit: Charles Craft

Heavy Duty

Canvas, duck and heavy denim blanks can be harder to embroider than those crafted from other fabrics, yet these sturdy totes and other accessories are popular and undeniably handy to use. Begin the search for solutions by analyzing the issues that arise with heavy fabric blanks: stiffness, impenetrability and weight.

Credit: The Sewphisticated Stitcher

Heavy blanks are often too stiff to turn inside out or arrange around the machine bed or needle bar. Even if a suitable arrangement is accomplished, once the hoop begins to move the stiff fabric around, its edges can bump the needle bar or slip under the needle to cause needle breakage. The heavier the fabric, the more alarming such missteps will seem.

Instead, open seams in the heavy blank to allow embroidery on a relatively flat and easily accessible single layer. If a hemmed edge is in the way, examine the blank to see whether the embroidery area can be approached from a different direction. For example, opening the side and bottom seams of a heavy tote allows easy access to the side panel without removing the upper hem or straps. And unlike the hem, these seams are usually without topstitching that can be hard to replace or reproduce.

Heavy fabrics can also make embroidery difficult by forming an almost impenetrable barrier to the needle. Conventional wisdom suggests using a larger needle with heavy fabrics, so switch to a size 90/14 embroidery needle. The needle's thicker shaft strengthens it as the needle punches through the heavy fabric. Titanium-coated needles may also improve stitch quality on heavy fabrics.

Sometimes an increase in needle size does not correct stitch problems. If the machine skips stitches with the larger needle, it may mean that the needle point is glancing off yarns in the fabric weave rather than piercing them. In that case, switch to a size 80/12 topstitching needle. Although its shaft is thinner, it is designed to protect the thread as it is carried through the fabric.

On the other hand, if the thread is shredding or breaking, a needle with a larger eye and deeper scarf, or groove, is needed. Choose a size 90/14 topstitching needle or even a size 100/16 for the heaviest fabrics.

One further effect of heavy fabric on embroidery is to cause a ragged, uneven appearance. The heavy yarns' texture causes the needle to slip toward the space

Self-adhesive templates can replace traditional marking techniques.
Credit: Floriani Template Tearaway

The Halloween patch has a secret: the facial features from the Large Bear design have been stitched with glow-in-the-dark thread!
Credit: Stitch A Logo

Credit: Zweigart, Stitch A Logo

between threads, as it may on loosely woven or highly textured fabrics. To counteract this effect, use a topper on the fabric right side and/or a heavy cutaway stabilizer underneath.

To minimize the effect of a heavy blank's weight during embroidery, arrange the work surface to supply plenty of support for the blank. This may mean moving the embroidery machine to a larger table, or arranging card tables or ironing boards beside and behind the machine table.

Also be sure the heavy item is securely hooped by checking the hoop's corners at every thread change. If the blank is too heavy to hoop, secure it to hooped stabilizer with both adhesive and basting stitches or pins placed well outside the embroidery area. Stay with the machine to catch any problems as soon as they arise.

Printable, semi-transparent template sheets make previewing design placement simple. They can also eliminate the need for marking the location on the blank, a real plus on hard-to-mark fabrics.

Many problems associated with embroidery on heavy blanks can be avoided by limiting the number of stitches that pass through the blank. While this could mean choosing smaller or less complex motifs, it can also be accomplished by creating a patch to apply to the heavy blank.

- ◆ Stitch the motif on stabilized fabric that coordinates with the blank. If desired, stitch a satin edging as the last part of the embroidered design.
- ◆ Trim the embroidered fabric outside the embroidery. Trim along the satin edging if there is one, or use a template to cut the embroidered material into a square, oval or other simple shape.

To apply the patch to the blank:

- ◆ Use temporary basting spray, glue stick or pins to position the satin-edged patch on the blank. With thread that matches the satin stitching, zigzag over the satin edge to attach the patch to the blank.
- ◆ Press under the edges of a raw-edge patch and position it on the blank as directed above. Use a straight stitch and thread that matches the patch fabric to sew the patch to the blank.
- ◆ Apply heavy-duty fusible web to the wrong side of the embroidered patch. Position the patch on the blank, cover with a press cloth and fuse in place. Alternately, use permanent glue instead of fusible web.

For patches that look the most like commercially available patch blanks, stitch words or motifs within a satin-edged frame. Work as if the patch fabric is an appliqué, with water-soluble stabilizer as the base fabric. Trim the patch fabric, but not the stabilizer, before stitching the satin outline. When the work is complete, rinse and soak the patch to remove the stabilizer, leaving a satin-edged patch.

Credit: All About Blanks

Woops!

Credit: Embroider This!

It's most likely to happen late in the day, just before deadline, within the last hundred stitches of a 300,000-stitch design. It's certainly happened to everyone who embroiders: a mistake, a goof, a machine problem, some malfunction that creates a glitch in the embroidered motif.

So what to do? Many times the problem can be corrected, sending you on your merry way to a lovely finished embroidery with no one the wiser. But how do you know when to say when, to give up on salvaging your embroidery project?

AVOIDING TROUBLE

The first line of defense is developing good work habits, and taking precautions to avoid the most common problems that occur during machine embroidery.

- Hoop securely, and double check the hoop every time you change threads to be sure the inner hoop doesn't spring free during embroidery. This is especially important with large, heavy or stiff materials, and when the hoop has been removed from the machine to change bobbins or trim appliqué shapes.

- Stay with the machine as it stitches, and watch the first few stitches carefully. Look for tension troubles, design misplacement (for example, upside down or incorrectly rotated) and incorrect thread color. If the problem is caught early, it's likely only a few understitches will need to be removed.

- Be aware of your body, and avoid bumping into the hoop. Also be sure the machine is positioned so the hoop will not hit a wall or other obstruction as the design stitches; this is especially important with oversized hoops.

- Try not to work when you are tired or distracted.

TO UNDO OR REDO?

Glitches can occur even when you are at your most diligent. Embroiderers are by nature a frugal crowd, so the temptation to take out stitches and start over – to salvage the project – is always strong.

Sometimes that's not the best strategy. If the design is being stitched on an inexpensive shirt that's easily replaced, it's not worth spending an hour to take out fill that stitched in twenty minutes. Replace the shirt instead.

On the other hand, if the work is part of an heirloom wedding dress, or if you are embroidering team logos on shirts and have no extra shirts on hand, it may be necessary to take out the stitches and redo. Take a break first, have a cup of tea or glass of water, maybe even take a walk; in other words, recharge yourself before beginning the tedious removal process.

- Use a fine seam ripper or small scissors that are sharp to the tip for cutting stitches that must be removed. A pair of fine tweezers that will grip embroidery thread securely is great for tugging stitches free of the fabric.

- Understitching and running stitches are usually easy to remove. Once most of the stitches are gone, use tweezers to gently pull and loosen the tie-off knots. Wide satin stitches are also easily removed by cutting through the bobbin threads, but remember they probably cover understitches that must also be removed.

- If only one color or a few stitches must be removed, leave the work in the hoop and be very careful not to alter the fabric's position in the hoop so the replacement stitches align properly.

- Remove the embroidery stitches while the stabilizer is still in place. It creates a barrier between the embroidery blank and the sharp tool used to cut the stitches.

- Work from the wrong side whenever possible while cutting stitches. Alternate from front to back as you pull the stitches with tweezers to remove the threads.

- Electric stitch removers and mustache trimmers (used upside down) can be used to shave off stitches for easier removal.

- A sharp craft knife or scalpel becomes an embroidery stitch remover when it is dragged broadside across the fabric surface. Alternate from front to back as you shave off stitches, and be sure you do not cut into the fabric itself.

SAVING THE UNSALVAGEABLE

The needle broke and tore a jagged hole in the fabric. After completing a large, closely filled motif, you discover that it's upside down. The fabric behaved unexpectedly, so the outlines are off. What now?

- Small holes in the fabric can be repaired. Cut a patch of permanent fusible interfacing larger than the hole. Arrange the fabric to fill the hole as completely as possible and cover the wrong side with the patch. Press to fuse. Complete the embroidery with a fresh piece of stabilizer, and the hole will disappear under the fill stitches.

- If the hole is located away from the embroidery design, as sometimes happens when a section of the blank becomes trapped under the embroidery hoop, patch it as above and cover the patch with a small embroidery motif related to the main design; for example, a bee to coordinate with a floral motif. Scatter other small motifs across the blank, if desired, for a more planned appearance.

- Restitch the embroidery motif on a separate piece of fabric that matches or coordinates with the original blank. Turn the edges under and slipstitch or topstitch the new design over the original, concealing the mistake.

Other patching options:

- Stitch the new design on lightweight, cut-away stabilizer. Trim the stabilizer a scant ¼" outside the embroidery. Turn the stabilizer to the wrong side as you hand stitch the motif to the blank, matching its location to the original embroidery. The result will be almost invisibly patched.

- Finish the replacement embroidery with a satin-stitch edge to make a patch, and use it as the new focal point on the blank.

- Back the patch with heavy-duty fusible web and iron it in place over the original motif. Follow the manufacturer's instructions for fusing, and you may find that the bond lasts longer than the blank itself!

Final Thoughts

Embellish a garment with all kinds of embroidery and other arts for a one-of-a-kind celebration.

Credit: Brother; various hand needlework patterns, stencils, and decorative machine stitches

As you experiment with the designs and ideas in this book and move forward with your own unique creations, remember that embroidery is a creative endeavor. It may be more mechanical than the stroke of a brush on canvas, but it's an art form nonetheless.

If you sell your work, charge an amount that compensates all the craft and business that machine embroidery encompasses. And when someone compliments your endeavor, smile and say "Thanks!" without qualifiers. In other words, don't say things like, "Oh, it's just machine work."

Remember that rules can be broken. If the monogram placement you have in mind isn't on "the list," don't let that deter you. When you have a stabilizer strategy that works for you every time, continue to use it even if "the book" (even this one!) recommends something different. There are infinite variables among threads, stabilizers, designs, machines and operators, and what works for you is as valid as any recommendation that's been proven by others.

Here's one final project idea, intended as a reminder of the fun that should accompany creativity. Select a denim shirt, vest, t-shirt or sweatshirt similar in fabric and weight to the blanks you most often embroider. Make sure it's your size.

Sometimes the most difficult part of embroidery is beginning, as questions of color and placement loom between the desire to stitch and the finished project. Use this garment to break through those roadblocks, as the canvas for test stitchouts, new stabilizer trials and thread experiments. Position designs anywhere and everywhere on the garment as you work on strategies for unconventional design placements. Use whatever color scheme suits the design or your mood of the day. Combine Christmas and Halloween motifs with Easter and Saint Patrick's Day.

If something doesn't go as planned, don't worry; you can cover it later with an embroidered patch. When it becomes obvious an experiment isn't working, you can stop in the middle of a design without finishing it. Don't wait until the garment is finished to wear your embroidered fun; the definition of finished is flexible here anyway. The point of this project is Anything Goes. Have Fun. Don't Worry.

At some point, before your wearable canvas is completely filled with design and color, take a few minutes to stitch this sentiment across the back or wherever you choose: Happy Everything!

That's what embroidery should be, as you fill in the blanks with color, style and fun.

Resources

BLANKS

All About Blanks
www.allaboutblanks.com
wide variety of blanks

Anita Goodesign
www.anita-goodesign.com
switch plate covers and embroidery
designs

Charles Craft
www.charlescraft.com
needlework fabrics and blanks

Crafter's Pride
www.crafterspride.com
800-277-6850
fabric and acrylic blanks

Embroider This!
www.embroiderthis.com
800-881-8144
variety of standard and unusual blanks

June Tailor
www.junetailor.com
no-sew pillow forms

Martha Pullen Company
www.marthapullen.com
smockables and heirloom blanks

Nature's Garden
www.naturesgardencards.com
handmade paper items

P. G. S. Specialties
www.pgsspecialties.com
877-242-6595
cards and paper blanks and project
instructions

ScrapSMART
www.scrapsmart.com
vinyl covers and printable imagery

Stitch A Logo
www.stitchalogo.com
www.blankpatch.com
818-956-3704
blank patches

The Sewphisticated Stitcher
www.thesewphisticatedstitcher.com
wide assortment of blanks

Walnut Hollow
www.walnuthollow.com
800-950-5101
wood blanks, clock kits

Wimpole Street
www.wimpolestreet.com
www.barrett-house.com
blank and embellished linens

**Wisconsin Lighting/Hollywood
Lights**
www.wilighting.com
800-657-6999
lampshades and bases to cover

Zweigart
www.zweigart.com
needlework fabrics and blanks

NOTIONS AND THREADS

Brother International
www.brothersews.com
800-422-7684
sewing/embroidery machines and
designs

Buzz Tools
www.buzztools.com
embroidery cataloging and editing
software

Coats & Clark
www.coatsandclark.com
embroidery and glow-in-the-dark
threads

"Designs in Machine Embroidery"
www.dzgns.com
Perfect Placement Kit and Perfect
Towel Kit

DMC
www.dmc-usa.com
cotton embroidery thread

Embroidery Arts
www.embroideryarts.com
Monogram Manager

Floriani Products/RNK Distributing
www.rnkdistributing.com
stabilizers and threads

Hoop-It-All
www.hoopitall.com
800-947-4911
stabilizers and Dry Cover-Up topper

Madeira
www.madeirausa.com
embroidery threads

Sulky of America
www.sulky.com
stabilizers and threads

The Warm Company
www.warmcompany.com
800-234-9276
battings and Steam-A-Seam 2

YLI
www.ylicorp.com
threads

EMBROIDERY DESIGNS

A Bit of Stitch
www.abitofstitch.com

A Time to Stitch
www.atimetostitch.com

Anita Goodesign
www.anita-goodesign.com

Criswell Embroidery & Design
www.k-lace.com

Deb Yedziniak Smockery
www.designsbythread.com

Embroidables
www.embroidables.com

Embroidery Arts
www.embroideryarts.com

Embroidery Library
www.emblibrary.com

In the Hoop Designs
www.inthehoopdesigns.com

My Embroidery Haven
www.myembroideryhaven.com

My Fair Lady Designs
www.myfairladydesigns.com

Oklahoma Embroidery Supply & Design (OESD)
www.embroideryonline.com

Sudberry House
www.machinecrossstitch.com

Sue Box
www.suebox.com

Vermillion Stitchery
www.vsccs.com

FURTHER READING

"Embroidery on Paper" by Annette Gentry Bailey

"Embroidery Machine Essentials" series by Jeanine Twigg et al

"Machine Embroidery Wild & Wacky" by Linda Turner Griepentrog and Rebecca Kemp Brent

"Machine Embroidery with Confidence" by Nancy Zieman
Krause Publications
888-457-2873
www.krausebooks.com

"Creative Machine Embroidery" magazine
www.cmemag.com

Diamond Threadworks
www.diamondthreadworks.com
embroidery placement charts and information

CD Contents

DESIGN NOTES

The embroidery designs on the enclosed CD-ROM are organized into folders by format. Look for the folder labeled with your machine's format and open it to find the designs for your use.

Design file names preceded by the letters "ABS" were digitized by Evy Hawkins at A Bit of Stitch. Those with "MFL" come from Shelly Smola at My Fair Lady Designs, and those with the letters "TTS" were created by Sherry Titzer at A Time to Stitch.

The enclosed CD-ROM also includes a folder labeled Design Information with files that include design sizes and thread colors. Please remember that any colors listed are only a suggestion, provided as an aid to visualizing which parts of a design are stitched with each thread change. Feel free to substitute other colors as you embroider a motif.

Several designs include appliquéd fabric. For these designs, the information file will also indicate when appliqué fabrics should be placed on the hoop or trimmed.

Some of the designs require a hoop larger than 4" x 4". For machines that do not have the appropriate large hoop, use customizing software such as BuzzEdit to divide the design into hoop-sized portions. The software can automatically insert registration marks, special stitches that are used as a guide for joining the design sections. Full-size templates can also be used for placing the design segments correctly. In addition, it may be necessary to convert the large size motif from a different file format after splitting the design.

Some items within the book were embroidered with only parts of a particular CD motif. An example is the coaster set on page 9. Use customizing or editing software to select portions of a design, and save the altered motif under a new name to preserve the original design.

Designs on CD

MFL-Baby Rattle

ABS Choo Choo Train

ABS Polar Bear Skating

Large Bear

MFL-Border 1

ABS Deco Frame

Cat 1

MFL-Baby Boy Design

MFL-Border 2

ABS Kittens Garden

Cat 2

MFL-Baby Design Blank

MFL-Corner 1

ABS Miss Priss Plain Oval

Cat 3

MFL-Baby Design with
Baby & Booties

MFL-Corner 2

ABS Miss Priss Scallop Oval

Cat 4

MFL-Baby Design with Booties

MFL-Paper Stipple 1

ABS Miss Priss Square Wave

Dots

MFL-Baby Girl Design

MFL-Paper Stipple 2

MFL-Paper Stipple 3

 MFL-Ring Bearer 2

 TTS Balloons

 TTS Santa Ltrs

 MFL-Paper Stipple 4

 Small Bear

 TTS Balloons Ltrs

 TTS Snow Angel

 MFL-Paper Stipple 5

 Snowflake 1

 TTS Bunny

 TTS Snow Angel Ltrs

 MFL-Paper Stipple 6

 Snowflake 2

 TTS Bunny Ltrs

 TTS Snowbaby

 MFL-Paper Stipple 7

 Snowflake 3

 TTS Ghost

 TTS Snowbaby Ltrs

 MFL-Paper Stipple 8

 Tin

 TTS Ghost Ltrs

 TTS Snowman

 MFL-Ring Bearer 1

 TTS All Sports Rnd

 TTS Santa

 TTS Snowman Ltrs

More Opportunities to Make the Most of Your Machine

BONUS CD-ROM with Every Book